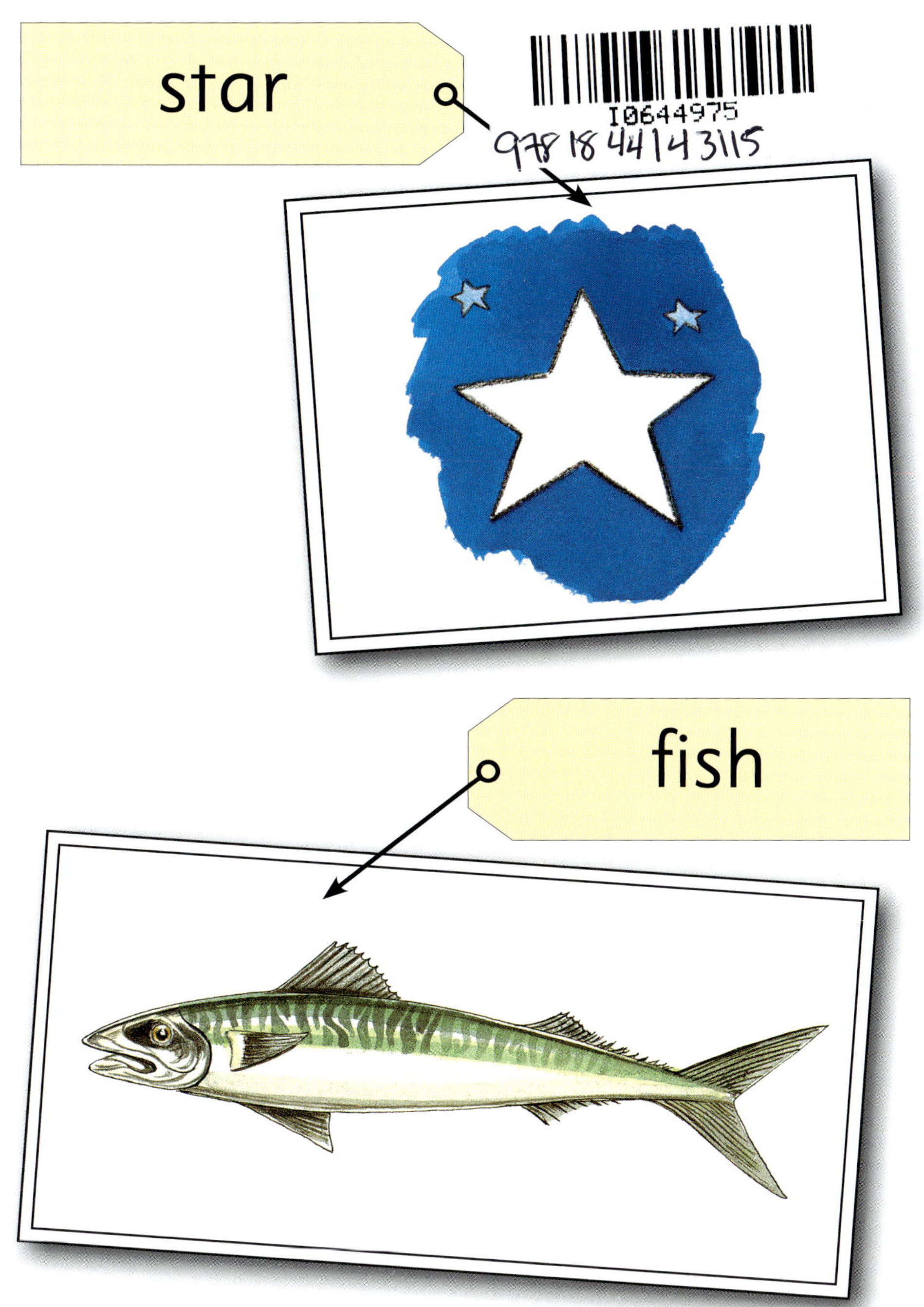
star
I0644975
9781844143115
fish

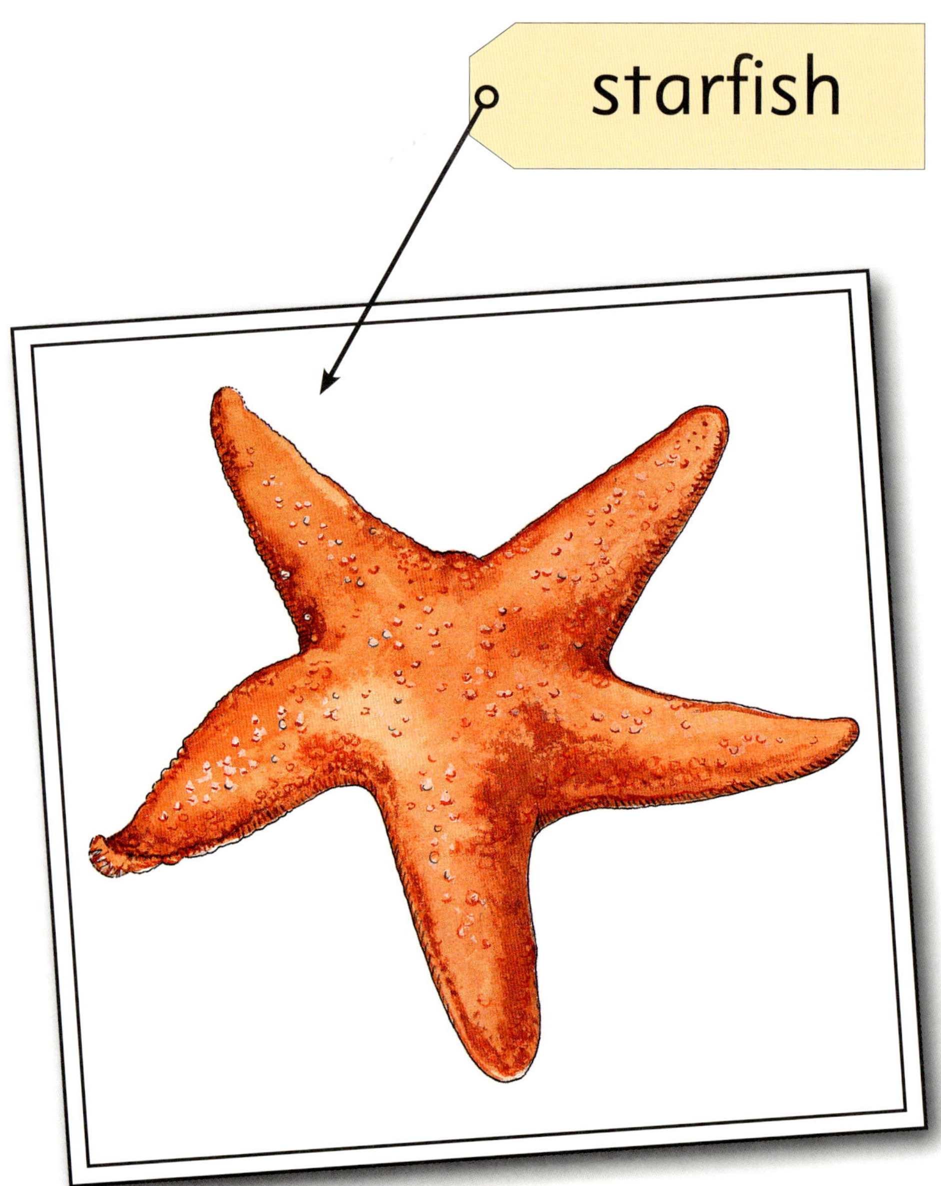
starfish

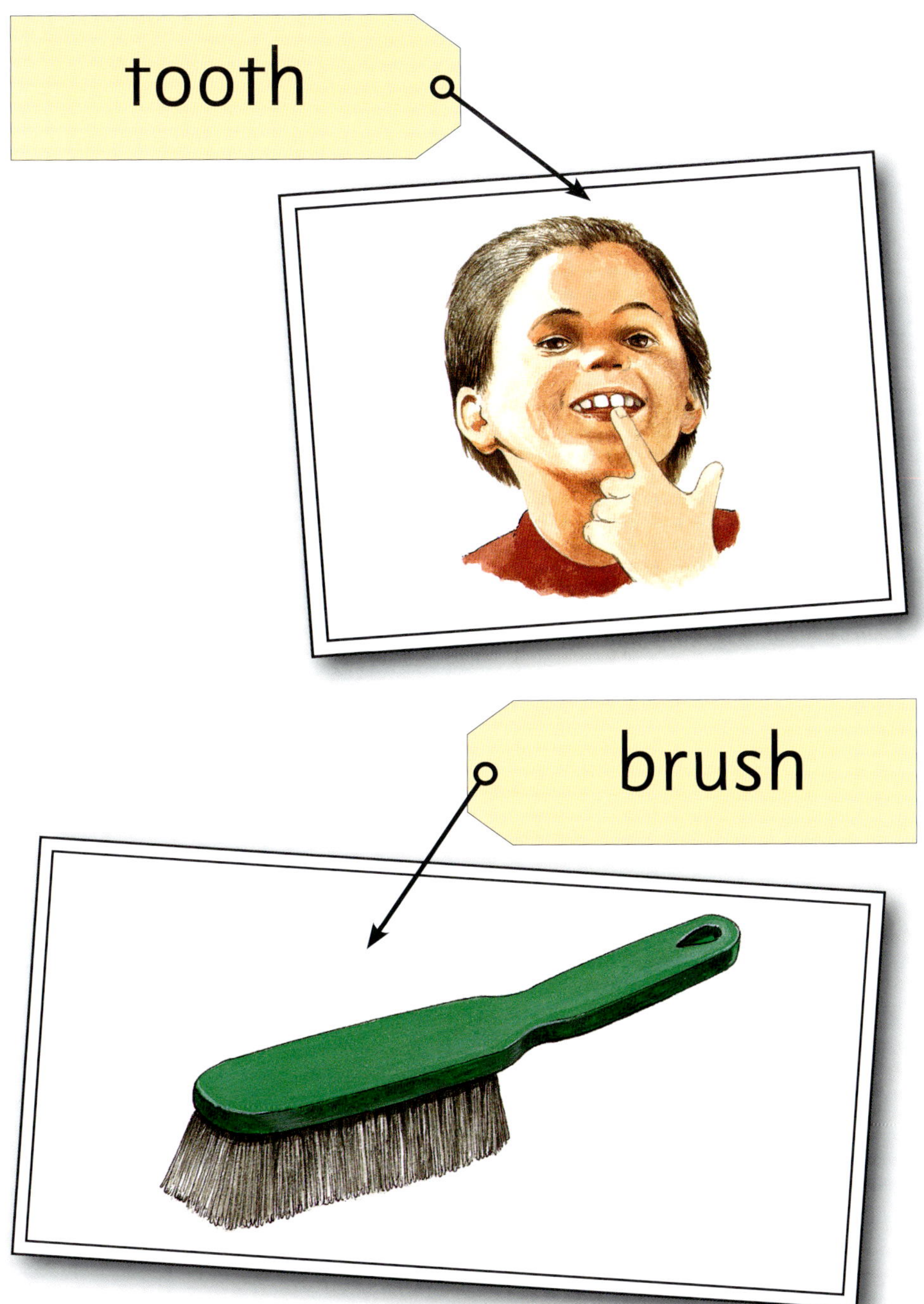
tooth
brush

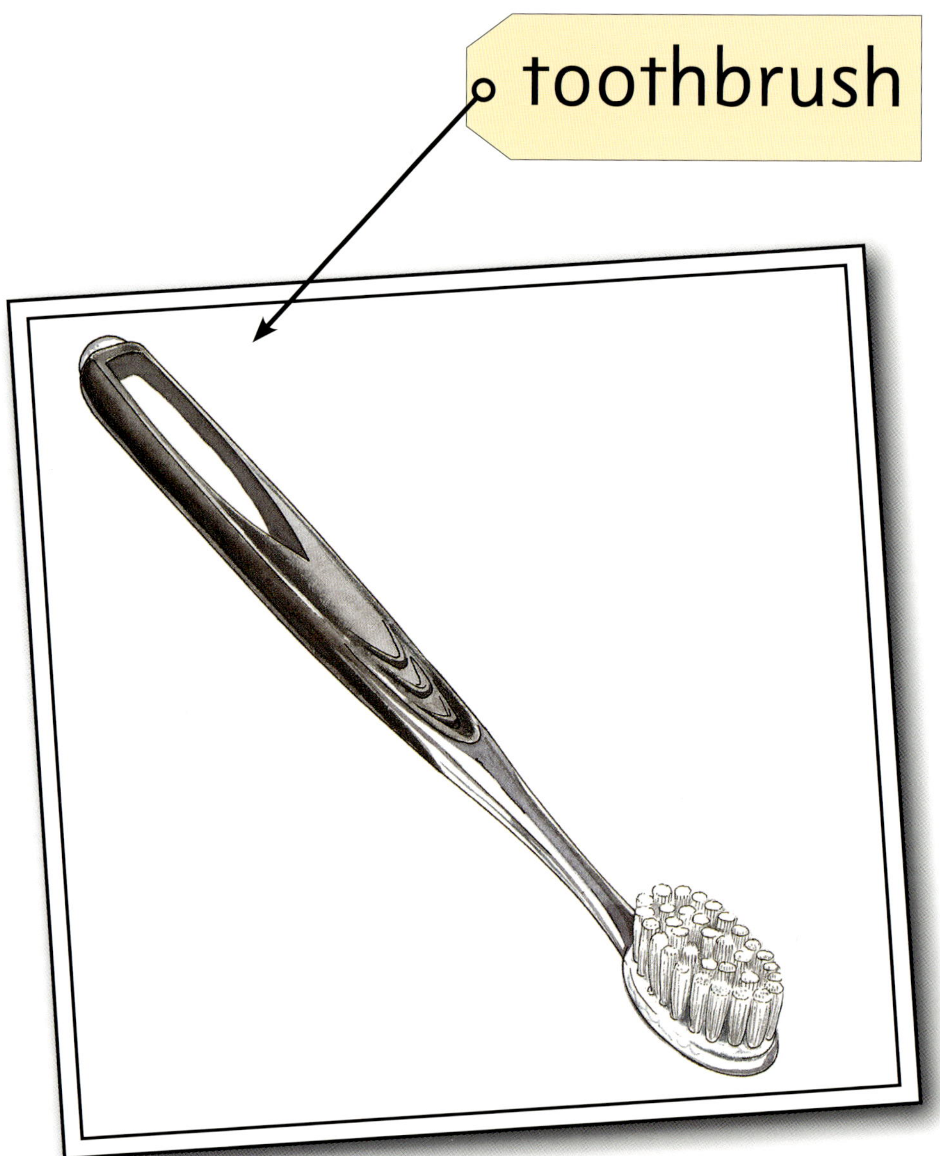
toothbrush

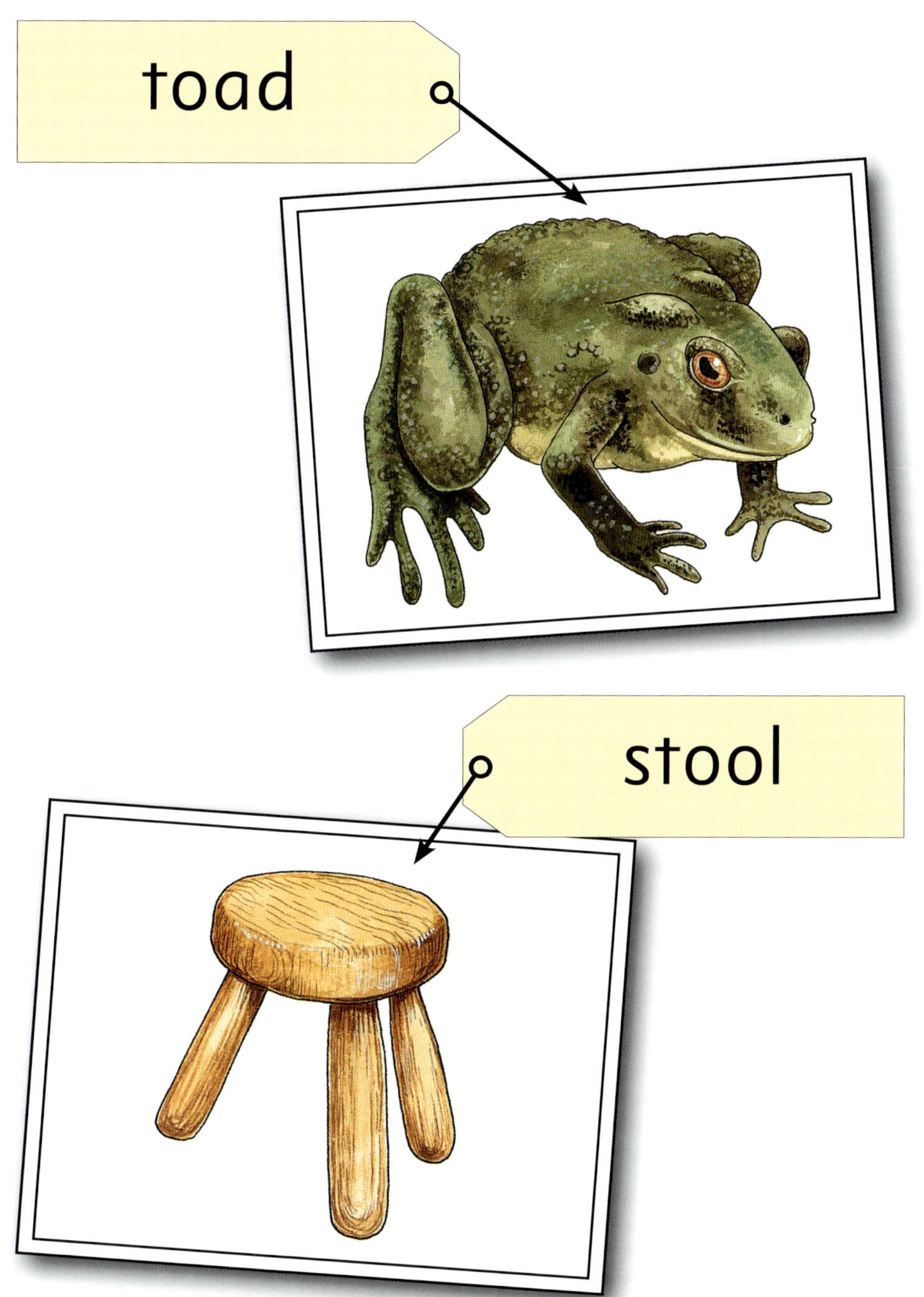
toad
stool

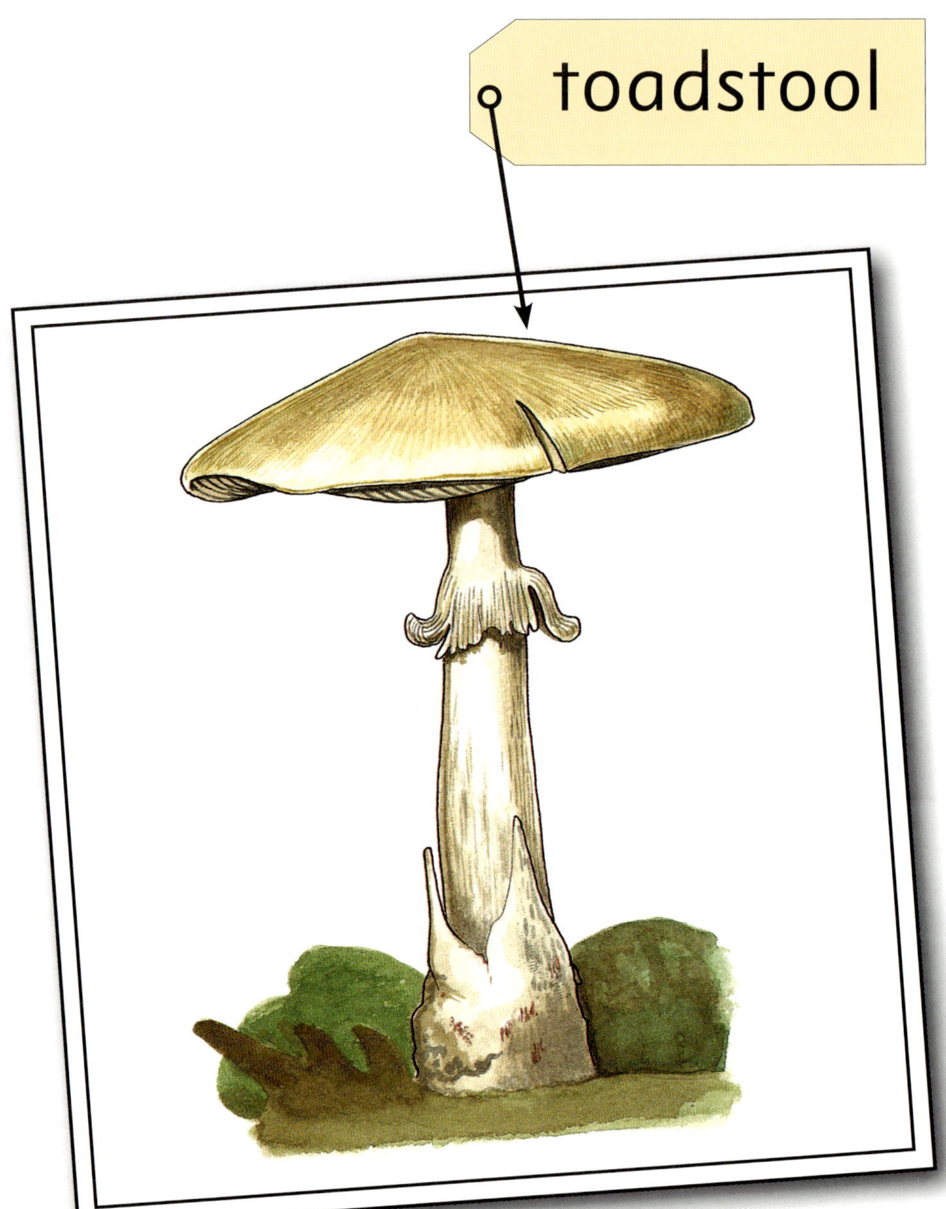
toadstool

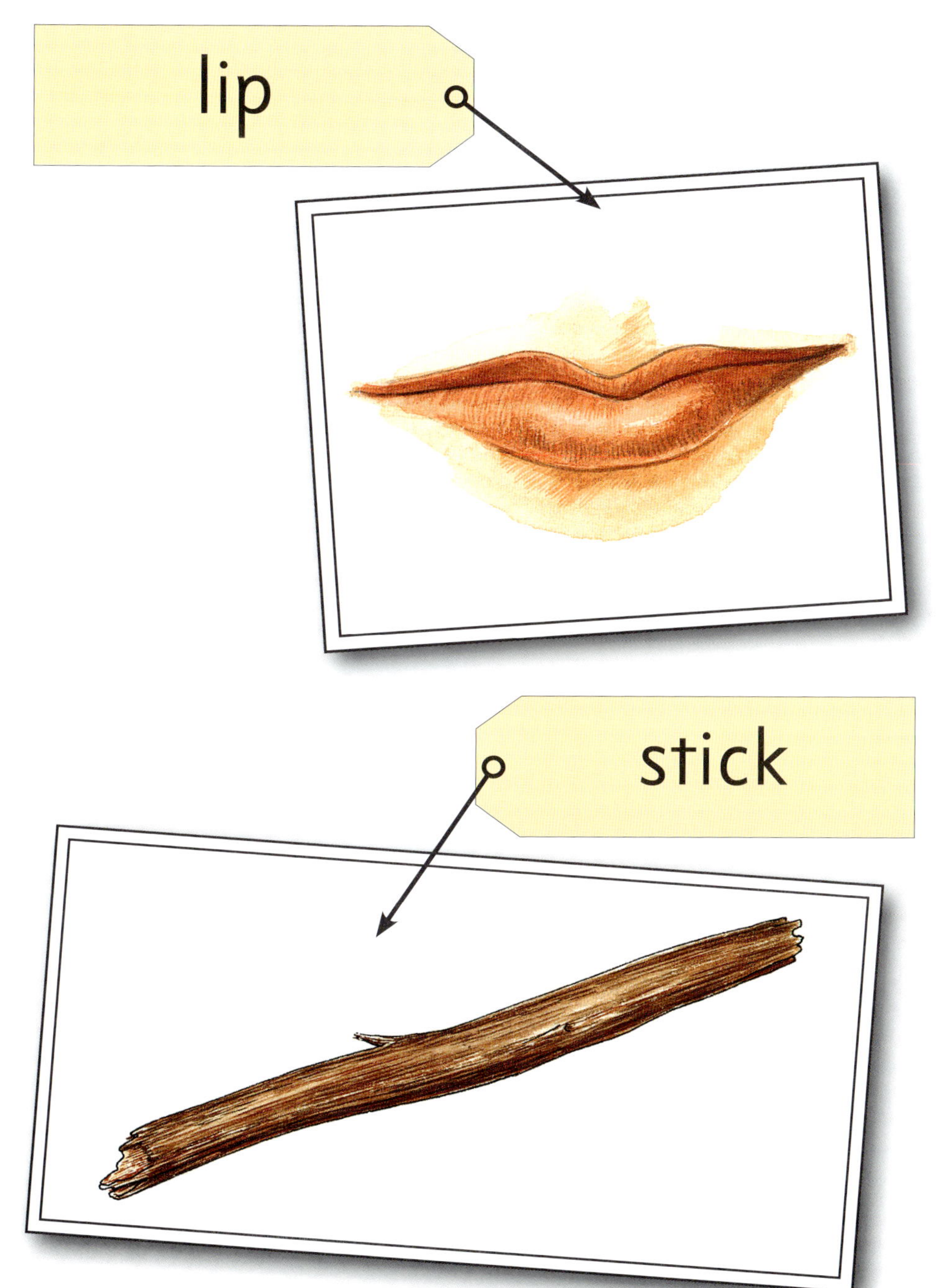
lip
stick

lipstick

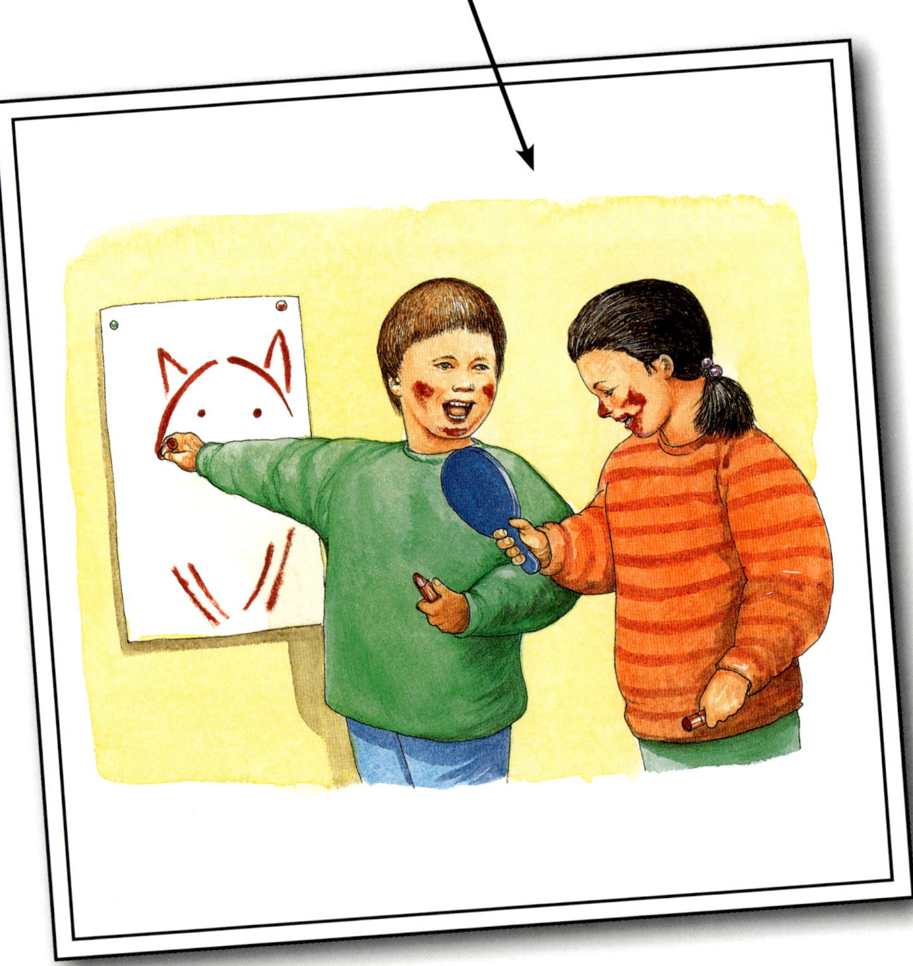